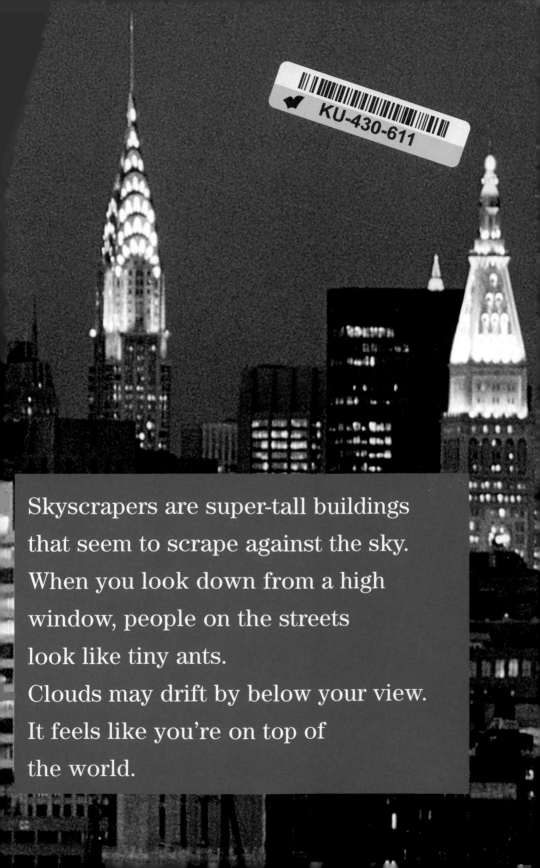

Skyscrapers are super-tall buildings
that seem to scrape against the sky.
When you look down from a high
window, people on the streets
look like tiny ants.
Clouds may drift by below your view.
It feels like you're on top of
the world.

This early skyscraper was built in Italy
more than 650 years ago.
It was built on soft ground.
Over the years it began to tilt to
one side.
We call it the Leaning Tower of Pisa.
We now know that skyscrapers need
a firm foundation to keep them
from sinking.

Today's skyscrapers would not
be possible without a strong
metal frame.
Early buildings could only
be 50 or 60 feet high because
the brick and stone walls had
to be very thick to support
the heavy weight of the
floors above.
Steel is so strong that a thin
cable can lift a cement truck.
And steel frames make it
possible to build skyscrapers
as tall as you want.

Steel is made by heating iron ore and small amounts
of coal and other substances in a large blast furnace.

The first modern skyscraper
was built in Chicago in 1885.
Soon, many cities began to
build skyscrapers.
These created a lot more
space for people to work and
live in the downtown areas.

The steel frame of the Reliance Building in Chicago
was put together in only four weeks.

The Empire State Building, in New York City, was completed in 1931.

It has a steel frame, concrete floors, and outside walls of brick and stone.

This 102-story building was the tallest in the world for 40 years.

It has more than 1,800 steps to the top.

It would take most people more than an hour to climb that high.

But high-speed elevators take you to the top in just a minute.

A skyscraper weighs thousands of tons.
It needs a firm foundation to keep
it from sinking into the ground
or falling over.
Hard, solid rock, called bedrock,
is best for a foundation.
Sometimes bedrock reaches to
the surface, but often it is buried
beneath soil or sand.
Steel or concrete columns called piles
are placed down through the softer
layers to bedrock.
If the bedrock is far beneath the
surface, a thick, wide slab of concrete
is used for the foundation.

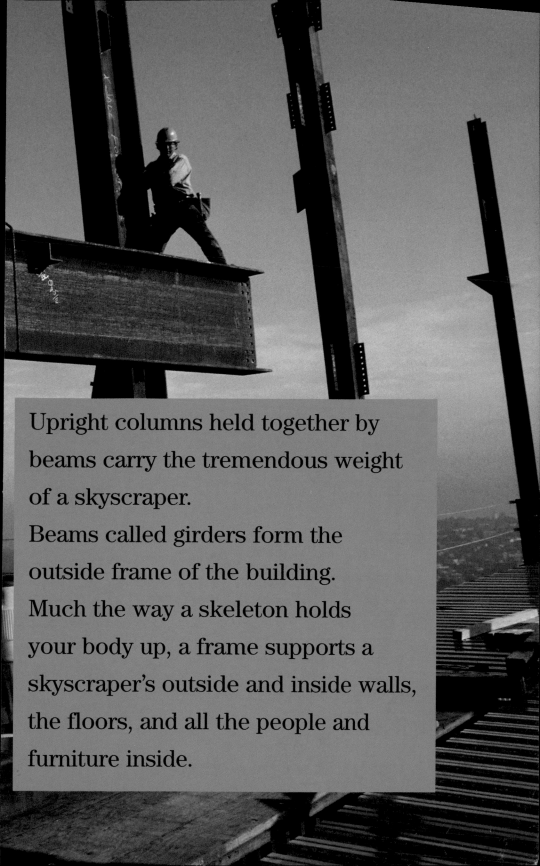

Upright columns held together by beams carry the tremendous weight of a skyscraper.
Beams called girders form the outside frame of the building.
Much the way a skeleton holds your body up, a frame supports a skyscraper's outside and inside walls, the floors, and all the people and furniture inside.

Many skyscrapers are built with
steel beams and columns.
Other skyscrapers are built with
concrete beams and columns
reinforced with steel rods.
Beams and columns are made in
different shapes.
Columns have a ⌶ shape
to help keep them from bending.
Beams have a I shape that allows
them to carry heavy weights.

People called ironworkers climb all over the framework of a skyscraper as if they are on a giant jungle gym. The workers walk along the narrow beams without fear of falling.
They fit beams and girders to the columns and bolt or weld them together.
These joints have to be just as strong as the beams and columns are themselves.

Cranes are powerful machines that lift materials from the ground up to where they are needed. Truck cranes that move on wheels are used at the start of construction. Then tower cranes do the lifting to higher floors. Tower cranes rise hundreds of feet into the air and can reach out just as far.

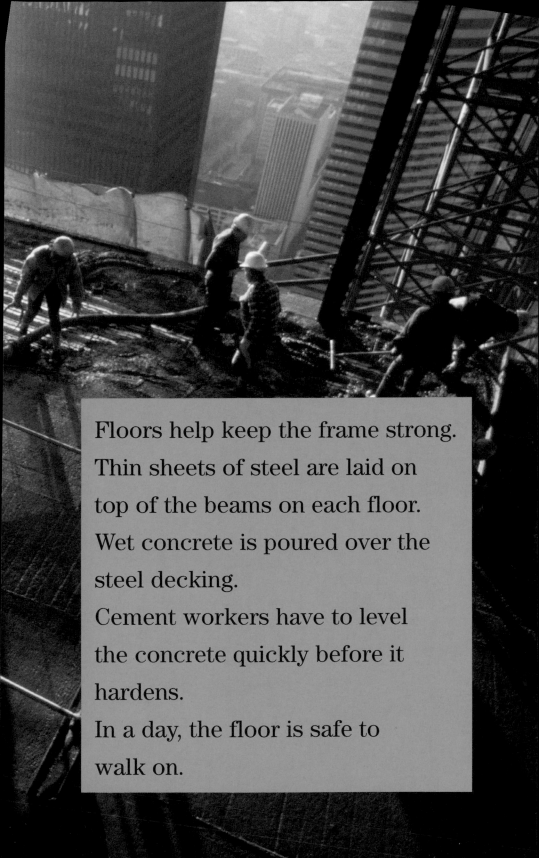

Floors help keep the frame strong.
Thin sheets of steel are laid on
top of the beams on each floor.
Wet concrete is poured over the
steel decking.
Cement workers have to level
the concrete quickly before it
hardens.
In a day, the floor is safe to
walk on.

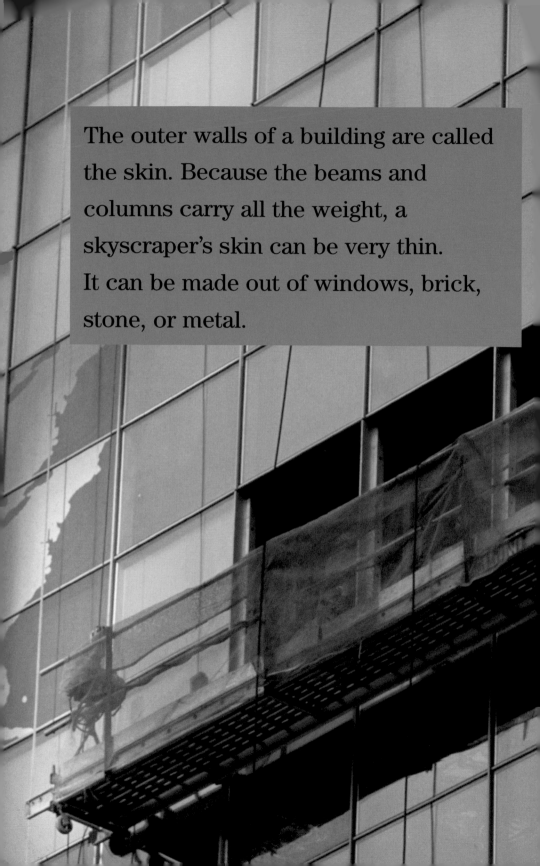

The outer walls of a building are called the skin. Because the beams and columns carry all the weight, a skyscraper's skin can be very thin. It can be made out of windows, brick, stone, or metal.

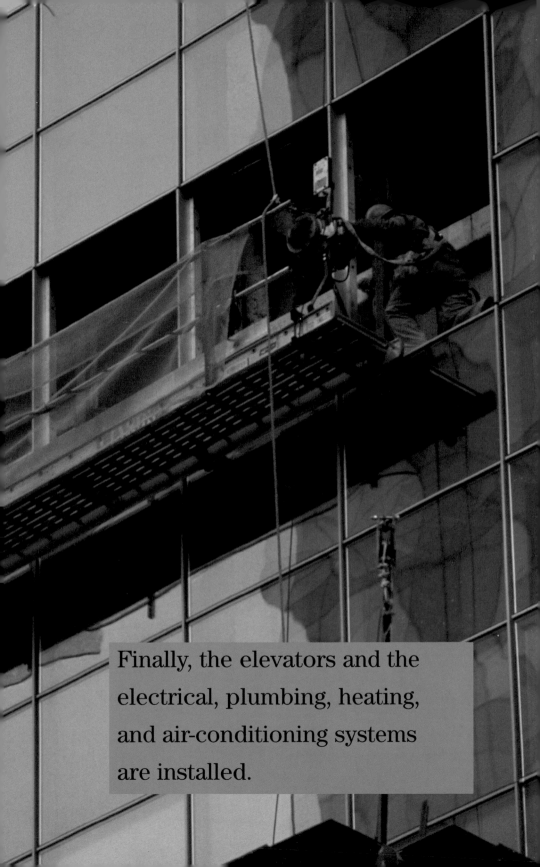

Finally, the elevators and the electrical, plumbing, heating, and air-conditioning systems are installed.

The Transamerica Pyramid in
San Francisco is 853 feet tall.
It is the only skyscraper in the world
built in the shape of a pyramid.
Three hundred miles of steel rods
were used to construct the
Transamerica Pyramid.
It takes a month to wash its
3,678 windows.

The Sears Tower in Chicago is 1,450 feet tall and has 110 floors.

It is about as tall as five football fields laid end to end.

When it was finished in 1973, it was the world's tallest building.

It is still the tallest building in North America.

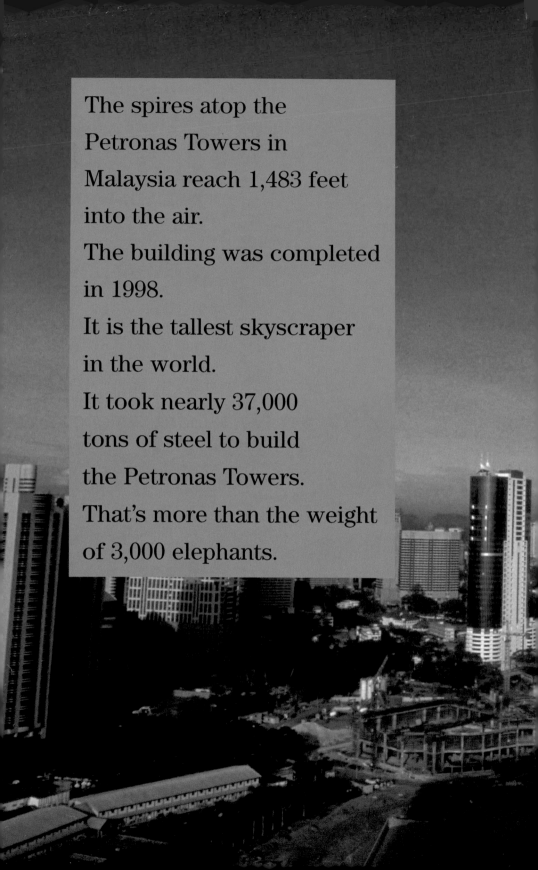

The spires atop the
Petronas Towers in
Malaysia reach 1,483 feet
into the air.
The building was completed
in 1998.
It is the tallest skyscraper
in the world.
It took nearly 37,000
tons of steel to build
the Petronas Towers.
That's more than the weight
of 3,000 elephants.

Someday, new skyscrapers will be
built that reach even higher into
the sky.
No one knows how high we can go.

Permission to use the following
photographs is gratefully
acknowledged:

Leaning Tower of Pisa ©
Massimo Borchi/Bruce Coleman
Inc.; Reliance Building courtesy
of Chicago Historical Society;
Empire State Building ©
Comstock.com; Transamerica
Pyramid © Lee Foster/Bruce
Coleman Inc.;
Sears Tower © Glenn
Short/Bruce Coleman Inc.;
Petrona Towers © Guy
Tillim/CORBIS SYGMA